American Lives

John Adams

Jennifer Blizin Gillis

Heinemann Library
Chicago, Illinois

© 2005 Heinemann Library
a division of Reed Elsevier Inc.
Chicago, Illinois

Customer Service 888-454-2279
Visit our website at www.heinemannlibrary.com

Designed by Heinemann Library
Photo research by Stephanie L. Miller
Printed and bound in China byWKT Company
Limited

09 08
10 9 8 7 6 5 4 3

Library of Congress Cataloging-in-Publication Data
Gillis, Jennifer Blizin, 1950-
   John Adams / Jennifer Blizin Gillis.
      v. cm. -- (American lives)
   Includes bibliographical references and index.
   Contents: Independence is born -- A happy
childhood -- Student, teacher, lawyer -- John and
Abigail -- A famous writer -- A difficult trial -- Tea
and trouble -- War breaks out -- In france --
Ambassador Adams -- Vice president Adams --
President Adams -- Full life.
   ISBN 1-4034-5959-2 (HB), 1-4034-5967-3 (Pbk.)
   ISBN 978-1-4034-5959-6 (HC)   978-1-4034-5967-1 (Pbk)
   1. Adams, John, 1735-1826--Juvenile literature. 2.
Presidents--United States--Biography--Juvenile
literature. [1. Adams, John, 1735-1826. 2.
Presidents.] I. Title. II. Series. III. Series: American
lives (Heinemann Library (Firm))
   E322.G55 2004
   973.4'4'092--dc22

                    2003027786

Acknowledgments
The author and publishers are grateful to the
following for permission to reproduce copyright
material:

Cover photograph by The Boston Athenaeum

Title page, pp. 5, 7, 8, 10, 16, 21 Bettmann/Corbis;
p. 4 Stock Montage; p. 9 Vermont Historical Society;
p. 11 Massachusetts Historical Society/The
Bridgeman Art Library; pp. 12, 24, 29 North Wind
Picture Archives; pp. 13, 23 Mary Evans Picture
Library; pp. 14, 18, 19, 22 National Archives and
Records Administration; pp. 15, 20r Massachusetts
Historical Society; p. 17 Corbis; pp. 20l, 25, 27
National Portrait Gallery/Smithsonian Institution/Art
Resource; p. 26 White House Historical Society; p.
28 Smithsonian American Art Museum, Washington,
DC/Art Resource

The publisher would like to thank Michelle Rimsa
for her comments in the preparation of this book.

Every effort has been made to contact copyright
holders of any material reproduced in this book.
Any omissions will be rectified in subsequent
printings if notice is given to the publisher.

The cover of this book shows a portrait of John Adams.
He was about 50 years old when it was painted.

Contents

Some words are shown in bold, **like this.** You can find out what they mean by looking in the glossary.

Independence Is Born

It is July 1, 1776. The Second **Continental Congress** is meeting to decide whether to declare independence from Great Britain. American soldiers are already fighting the British. Colonists worry that British warships will attack.

A committee has written the **Declaration of Independence.** Congress only needs to vote on it. Then the thirteen colonies will form a new, independent government. But the lawmakers won't stop arguing.

John Adams wrote that July 2, not July 4, would be remembered as "Independence Day." But the Declaration of Independence was approved on July 4, so that is the day we celebrate.

On this hot, damp morning John Adams begins to speak. Thunder and lightning rattle the windows, but John speaks on. He tells the people in the room how important this decision will be. It will affect the lives of people who aren't even born yet. It is time for everyone to stop thinking about today and start thinking about the future.

The next day, Congress votes. Thanks to John's two-hour speech, the colonies declare their independence.

This picture of John Adams was painted when he was about 30 years old.

A Happy Childhood

John Adams was born on October 30, 1735 in Braintree, Massachusetts. John loved his parents very much. His father, Deacon John Adams, was a shoemaker and farmer. He was very religious. When John got older, he wrote about how kind his father was to him.

John learned to read at home. Then he went to a small school in a neighbor's house. He was very smart and loved to talk. John's brother Peter said he was "the talkingest boy" he ever knew.

Massachusetts was one of America's original thirteen colonies. John was born in a part of Braintree that became part of a town called Quincy.

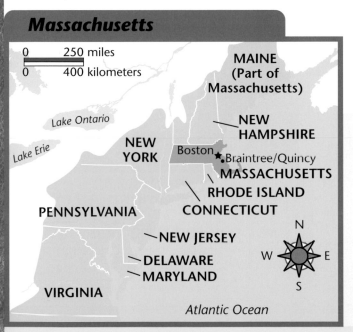

Massachusetts

0 250 miles
0 400 kilometers

Lake Ontario
Lake Erie
MAINE (Part of Massachusetts)
NEW HAMPSHIRE
NEW YORK
Boston ★ Braintree/Quincy
MASSACHUSETTS
RHODE ISLAND
CONNECTICUT
PENNSYLVANIA
NEW JERSEY
DELAWARE
MARYLAND
VIRGINIA
Atlantic Ocean

N W E S

The Life of John Adams

1735	1764	1770	1776
John Adams is born on October 30	*Marries Abigail Smith*	*Defends British soldiers involved in the Boston Massacre*	*Talks **Continental Congress** into voting for independence*

John grew up with two younger brothers in the house on the right. When he got married, he and his wife moved into the house on the left. In John's time, fields surrounded the houses.

When John got older, he started school. One day, he told his father that he wanted to quit school and be a farmer. John's father hoped John would become a minister, so he wanted John to stay in school. When John was fifteen, he took a test to get into Harvard College in Cambridge, Massachusetts.

1785	1789	1796	1818	1826
Becomes first U.S. **Ambassador** to Great Britain	Becomes Vice President of the United States	Elected President of the United States	Abigail dies	John dies on July 4

Student, Teacher, Lawyer

Harvard College trained ministers. But John soon decided he would rather be a lawyer. He took a teaching job to earn money to study law.

John was sixteen when he went to Harvard. He was one of the three best students there. After graduation, John got a job teaching in a one-room school. John wrote in his journal that he liked the students, but he did not like having to keep order in the class.

John began to study law in 1756. In those days, people who wanted to be lawyers spent time studying with another lawyer. Then, if they passed a test called the bar exam, they could open their own law business.

John studied with a lawyer for two years. He passed his bar exam in 1759. But John lost his very first court case. He was embarrassed. He decided to spend extra time studying to be a better lawyer.

All his life, John wrote about people and places around him. He wrote many letters to his friends and family. While at Harvard College, he also started writing in a journal.

John and Abigail

In 1764, John married Abigail Smith. They moved into the house where John had his law business. Abigail came from a respected family. Her father was a minister. Abigail liked to talk and read almost as much as John did! In those days, that was very unusual.

This picture of Abigail was painted soon after she and John married. From her letters, we know that she was a strong and independent woman.

John and Abigail loved each other very much. During their 54-year marriage, they often had to be apart because of John's work. But they wrote long letters to each other that tell us a lot about life in the 1700s.

This picture of John was painted when he was about 30 years old. John loved to eat, and Abigail sometimes teased him about his weight.

Sons and Daughters

John and Abigail had six children. Susanna and Elizabeth died when they were babies. John Quincy became the sixth president of the United States.

- *Abigail (called Nabby)   born 1765*
- *John Quincy   born 1767*
- *Susanna   born 1768*
- *Charles   born 1770*
- *Thomas Boylston   born 1772*
- *Elizabeth   born 1777*

A Famous Writer

In 1765, John Adams wrote an article for a Boston newspaper. It said that Americans had a right to be free and think for themselves. John's name was not on the article, but people soon found out he wrote it. Some people said it was the best article they had ever read.

Great Britain had put a **tax** on almost every piece of paper the colonists used. Adams wrote to the Massachusetts **legislature.** He told the lawmakers that Great Britain did not have the right to tax the colonists.

The British tax on paper was called the Stamp Tax. Colonists had to pay for a stamp like this on almost every piece of paper they used—including playing cards!

This picture shows Boston Harbor in its early days.

In 1767 Great Britain put taxes on tea, paint, and glass. In 1768 Adams moved his law office and his family to Boston. That year, Great Britain sent soldiers to Boston to keep the colonists from causing trouble. Adams was getting very angry about the way Great Britain was treating the colonists.

A Difficult Trial

In the fall of 1770, Adams had his most famous court case. He spoke for British soldiers who had killed colonists during the Boston Massacre. This was dangerous for Adams to do. Some colonists thought he was helping the British. Some even wanted to harm him and his family.

Adams believed that everyone should have a fair trial. But the facts were very confusing. Some **witnesses** against the soldiers had not even been at the riot. Adams was careful not to make them look foolish. He did not want angry colonists to start more trouble.

In March 1770, a group of colonists was yelling at some British soldiers. The soldiers thought they heard an order to shoot their guns. They killed five people. Angry colonists called this a massacre, meaning that the soldiers had killed people for no reason.

John Adams made these notes during the Boston Massacre trial. He blamed Great Britain for the riots, not the soldiers. Most of the soldiers were set free.

Worrying about the trial was not good for Adams 's health. When it was over, he moved his family back to Braintree. He spent hours writing down his thoughts about government and peoples' rights.

First Continental Congress

In 1774, Adams was a **representative** at the first **Continental Congress.** It was a meeting of lawmakers from twelve **colonies.** For the first time, they were planning to work together to see what they could do about Great Britain.

Adams helped write up complaints against Great Britain. **Taxes** were at the top of the list. Lawmakers also disagreed with the way Great Britain tried to control the colonists by sending warships and forcing them to let soldiers stay in their homes.

In 1773, the people of Boston were angry about a tax on tea. Some of them dressed as Native Americans and dumped tea into the harbor. This became known as the Boston Tea Party.

Adams said that people are born with the right to live and be free. No one, not even a king, could take these rights away. The lawmakers decided that the colonies would not buy anything from Great Britain or any of its other colonies.

The first Continental Congress met at Carpenter's Hall in Philadelphia, Pennsylvania in September of 1774.

War Time

The battle at Lexington was near Braintree. John Quincy and Abigail watched some of the fighting from a hill near their farm.

In April 1775, the **Revolutionary War** began in Lexington, Massachusetts. Adams was away at the Second **Continental Congress.** He worked very hard for the thirteen American **colonies** to become independent.

He helped organize a navy. He helped write the **Declaration of Independence.** His hardest job was to make sure that all the soldiers fighting for independence had enough weapons, food, and other supplies.

Three Branches

Adams thought the new government should have three parts, or branches. Each of the three branches would keep any one of the others from becoming too strong and taking over the country.

- *A legislative branch to make laws for the country*
- *A judicial branch, or system of courts, to make sure the laws are fair and are carried out*
- *An executive branch, or president, to oversee things and make sure all government branches work together*

At the same time, Adams wrote newspaper articles and a booklet about government. These helped colonists think about how their new country would be ruled when it became independent from Great Britain.

The Continental Congress voted to declare independence from Great Britain on July 2, 1776. The written Declaration of Independence was approved on July 4. The people of Philadelphia heard the declaration on July 8, 1776.

In France

John Adams went to France twice. In 1778, he went to ask for help with the **Revolutionary War.** It was a very dangerous trip. The ship ran into a storm and almost sank. They had to fight off some British warships. In those days, it usually took three or four weeks to sail to France. This trip took over six weeks!

Adams loved Paris. He and Benjamin Franklin met lots of important people. Adams even met with King Louis XVI.

Adams took his son John Quincy with him to France. John Quincy made these drawings of ships he saw along the way.

Adams returned home in August 1779. He then helped write the **constitution** for the state of Massachusetts.

Congress sent Adams back to France in November. They wanted him to help talk the British into ending the war. Adams was still there when the Revolutionary War ended in 1783. A few years later, Abigail came to France to be with him.

Abigail brought their oldest daughter, Nabby, to France with her. The style then was for women to look pale and wear powdered wigs.

Historical Writings

The Massachusetts constitution is the oldest written constitution in the world that is still being followed.

Ambassador Adams

John and Abigail Adams stayed in France for a year. In 1785, Adams became U.S. **ambassador** to Great Britain. The Adams family moved to a large house in London.

Very few people in Great Britain were friendly toward Adams. They were still angry with Americans because of the **Revolutionary War.** The United States needed to earn money by selling things to the British. But the British would not let any American ships into their ports. They also refused to close their forts in some parts of the United States.

This painting shows Adams when he was ambassador to Great Britain. He was the U.S. ambassador to Holland at the same time.

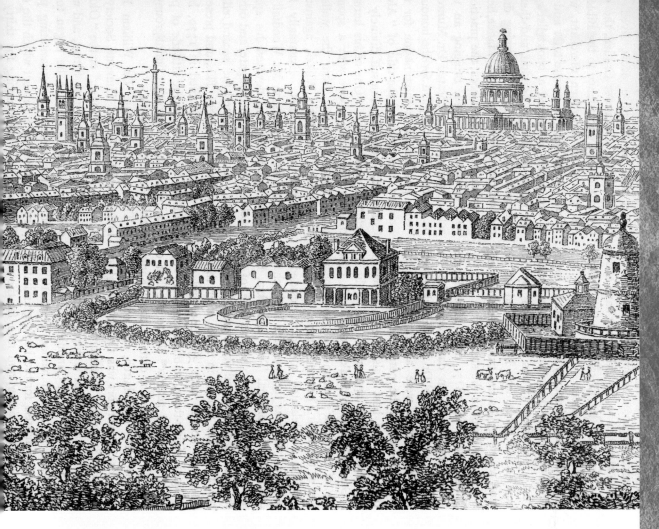

In the 1780s, London may have been the busiest city in the world. About one million people lived there. John Adams and his family often went to concerts and the theater.

Adams and his family went back to Massachusetts in 1788. Adams had been away from home, and away from some of his children, for eight years.

Vice President Adams

John Adams had always been popular in Massachusetts. When he and his family returned from England, Adams was welcomed as a **Revolutionary War** hero. Cheering crowds met him at his ship, and church bells were ringing.

George Washington was elected president of the United States in 1789. Adams was elected vice president. Right away, he got into trouble.

Some of the Adams children had lived with relatives while John was in France and England. The family was rejoined when they moved to this house, called Peacefield.

Adams thought people should call the president "Your Excellency" or "His Highness." He wore such fancy clothes to Congress that people made fun of him. He argued with his old friend Thomas Jefferson over the way the government should be organized, and they stopped speaking to each other.

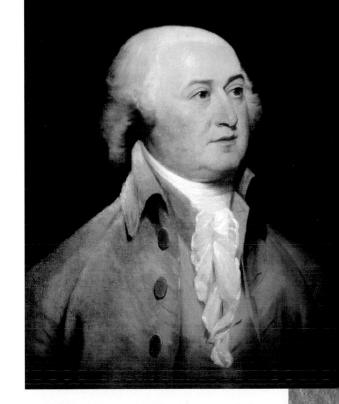

Adams was 53 years old when he became vice president. He complained in his writings that he did not think it was a very important job.

Tie Breaker

As vice president, Adams was the head of the U.S. Senate. If there is a tie vote on any law, the head of the Senate can vote to break the tie. During his vice presidency, Adams did this over 30 times! That is more than any other vice president since.

President Adams

In 1796, John Adams was elected president of the United States. Thomas Jefferson became vice president. Jefferson and Adams often did not agree with each other. They had different ideas about many things.

There was trouble outside the government, too. France was at war with Great Britain. French ships began attacking American ships and capturing American sailors. Many people wanted the United States to go to war against France, but Adams worked hard for peace.

Adams was the first president to live in the White House. It was still not finished when they moved in. Abigail used the East Room to dry their laundry! Today, the East Room is one of the most beautiful rooms in the White House.

A famous artist named Gilbert Stuart painted this picture of Adams. Adams was about 64 years old when it was painted.

Adams was not a very popular president. He signed a bill that said people could be put in prison if they wrote or said anything against the U.S. government. Then Congress passed a **tax** to help the United States build an army and a navy. Many people thought this went against everything they had fought for in the **Revolutionary War.**

A Full Life

Adams ran for president again in 1800, but he lost to Thomas Jefferson. Adams went home to Massachusetts thinking he would die soon. He was 65 years old, and most people did not live much past 50 or 60 in those days.

But Adams lived many more years. He lived to make friends with Thomas Jefferson again. The two men wrote letters back and forth for fourteen years.

Gilbert Stuart painted this picture of Adams when he was 89 years old. People said that the painting showed his true spirit.

He lived to see his son John Quincy become the sixth president of the United States. And, when Adams was in his 80s, he still went on three-mile (almost five-kilometer) walks.

As Adams got older, Abigail was often sick. Just after Adams's 83rd birthday, Abigail got **typhoid fever.** She died on October 28, 1818.

On July 4, 1826, Adams was sick in bed. From outside came the sounds of celebration. It was the 50th anniversary of the first Independence Day. Late in the day, Adams said, "Thomas Jefferson survives." But he was wrong. Adams and his old friend died just a few hours apart on the same day.

John, Abigail, John Quincy, and his wife are all buried at United First Parish Church in Quincy, Massachusetts.

Glossary

ambassador   person who speaks and acts for the government of a country

colony   group of people who move to another land but are still ruled by the country they came from. People who live in a colony are called colonists.

constitution   set of laws for a state or country

Continental Congress   group of men that spoke and acted for the colonies that became the United States. It was formed to deal with complaints about Great Britain.

Declaration of Independence   document that said the United States was an independent nation. Independent means not under the control or rule of another person or government.

legislature   group of lawmakers in a colony or state

representative   person who is chosen to act or speak for a group of people

Revolutionary War   war from 1775 to 1783 in which American colonists won their freedom from Great Britain

Senate   one of two groups of lawmakers that make up the U.S. Congress

tax   money people must pay to the government

typhoid fever   disease caused by germs that spread quickly from one person to another, killed many people at a time, and for which there was no cure

witness   person in a court case who tells what he or she saw or heard happen

More Books to Read

Behrman, Carol H. *John Adams*. Minneapolis, Minn.: Lerner, 2004.

Feinberg, Barbara. *John Adams*. Danbury, Conn.: Children's Press, 2003.

Marcovitz, Hal. *John Adams*. Broomall, Penn.: Mason Crest, 2003.

Santella, Andrew. *John Adams*. Mankato, Minn.: Compass Point, 2003.

Places to Visit

Adams National Historical Park
135 Adams Street
Quincy, MA 02169-1749
Visitor Information: (617) 770-1175

Freedom Trail
Boston National Historical Park Visitors' Center
15 State Street
Boston, MA 02109
Visitor Information: (617) 242-5642

Index